FENCING

Jessica Coupé

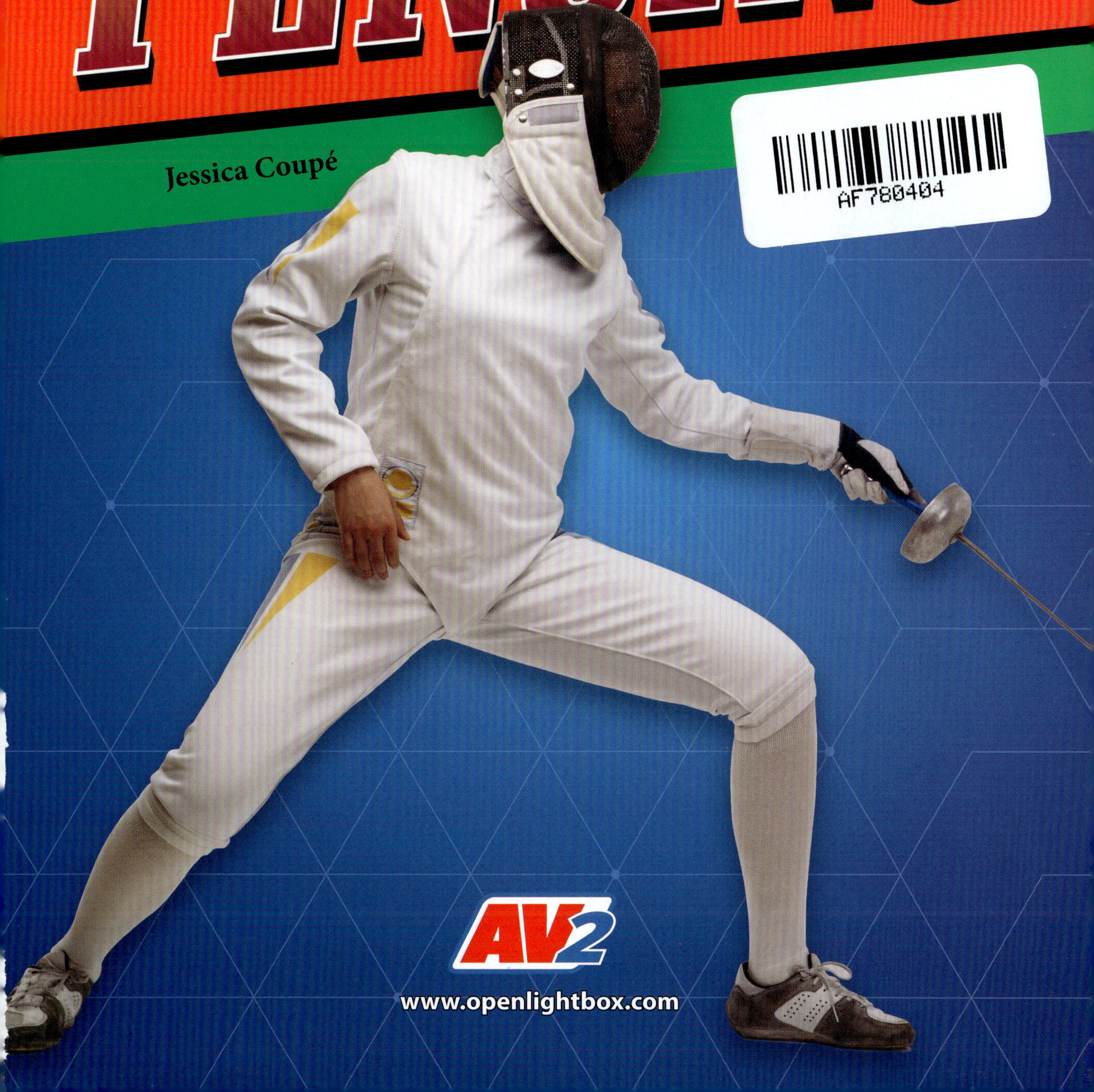

AV2
www.openlightbox.com

Step 1
Go to **www.openlightbox.com**

Step 2
Enter this unique code
WSPQZCVSL

Step 3
Explore your interactive eBook!

AV2 is optimized for use on any device

Your interactive eBook comes with...

Contents
Browse a live contents page to easily navigate through resources

Audio
Listen to sections of the book read aloud

Videos
Watch informative video clips

Weblinks
Gain additional information for research

Slideshows
View images and captions

Try This!
Complete activities and hands-on experiments

Key Words
Study vocabulary, and complete a matching word activity

Quizzes
Test your knowledge

Share
Share titles within your Learning Management System (LMS) or Library Circulation System

Citation
Create bibliographical references following APA, CMOS, and MLA styles

This title is part of our AV2 digital subscription

1-Year Grades K–5 Subscription
ISBN 978-1-7911-3320-7

Access hundreds of AV2 titles with our digital subscription.
Sign up for a FREE trial at **www.openlightbox.com/trial**

FOR THE LOVE OF SPORTS

FENCING

CONTENTS

What Is Fencing?

Today, fencing is considered one of the safest sports. Fencers wear protective equipment over their entire bodies.

The sport of fencing developed from sword combat. Ancient **civilizations**, such as the Egyptians, Greeks, and Romans, used swords when they went to war. The ways in which swords were used changed over time. By the **Renaissance**, European swordfighting was seen in both war and sport, including fencing. Eventually, fencing schools opened across Europe.

By the 1800s, fencing had standardized rules, weapons, and equipment. Fencers usually specialized in one of three weapons—the **saber**, the **épée**, or the **foil**. Two fencers would compete against each other, trying to get points, or **touches**, by striking their opponent in a target area on the uniform.

Fencing was one of nine sports included in the first modern Olympic Games in Athens, Greece, in 1896. Leon Pyrgos, Eugène-Henri Gravelotte, and Ioannis Georagiadis won gold medals in the sport that year. Today, fencing continues to be a popular sport worldwide. It has fans and competitors in more than 100 countries around the world. At the 2024 Olympics, 212 fencers competed across 12 events. Many people enjoy watching fencing during the Olympics and other worldwide competitions.

Fencers often start competing professionally after 2 to 3 years of training and practice.

The earliest evidence of fencing comes from Egyptian wall paintings created in 1190 BC.

The longest recorded fencing match, in 2016, lasted 11 hours and 40 minutes.

In 2019, "lightsaber fencing," from the Star Wars movies, was officially recognized as a sport by the French Fencing Federation.

Getting Ready to Play

Each weapon used in fencing has a unique structure. The épée is a long, heavy sword that has a large **guard** on the handle. The foil has a flexible blade up to 43 inches (110 centimeters) long, and weighs up to about 1.1 pounds (500 grams). The saber is shorter than the foil or épée, but can be used for slashing.

Fencers wear a uniform that keeps them safe and helps record when they are hit by an opponent. It is made of a thick fabric that covers the body from head to foot. Fencers wear a jacket made of a strong material, such as Kevlar. A mask made of a strong **mesh** protects the face and head.

Electronic scoring equipment is often used to keep track of hits. A scoring machine uses red, green, and yellow or white lights to show if a fencer gets a hit.

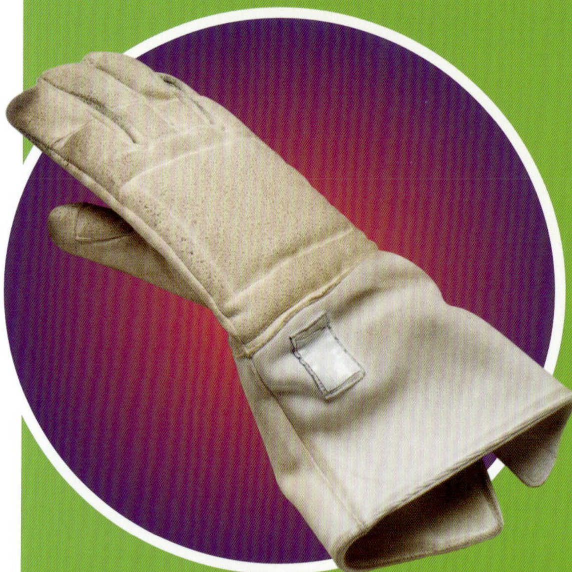

A thick glove covers a fencer's weapon hand. It protects the fencer from cuts or bruises during competitions.

If a sword is to be used in competitions with electronic scoring, it must have a socket to connect to scoring equipment.

The wire mesh used in fencing masks have gaps of less than 0.1 inches (0.2 cm). The masks are often made of stainless steel.

Today's fencers wear a jacket called a lamé. It is lined with metal wires that register a hit when struck by a weapon connected to the electronic scoring system.

Fencers wear a pad called a plastron under their jackets. This protects the upper body from injury.

The Piste

A fencing match takes place in an area called a piste or strip. It is 46 feet (14 meters) long. The piste is marked with several lines. A center line splits the piste in half, while en garde lines determine starting positions. Warning lines let fencers know if they are approaching rear limit lines, which award a point to the opponent when crossed.

In some events, each fencer's jacket is attached to a cord. The other end of the cords are on **reels** at each end of the piste. The reels hold 66 feet (20 m) of cable. The cables allow the electronic scoring system to recognize touches. In competitions with wireless scoring systems, reels are not needed.

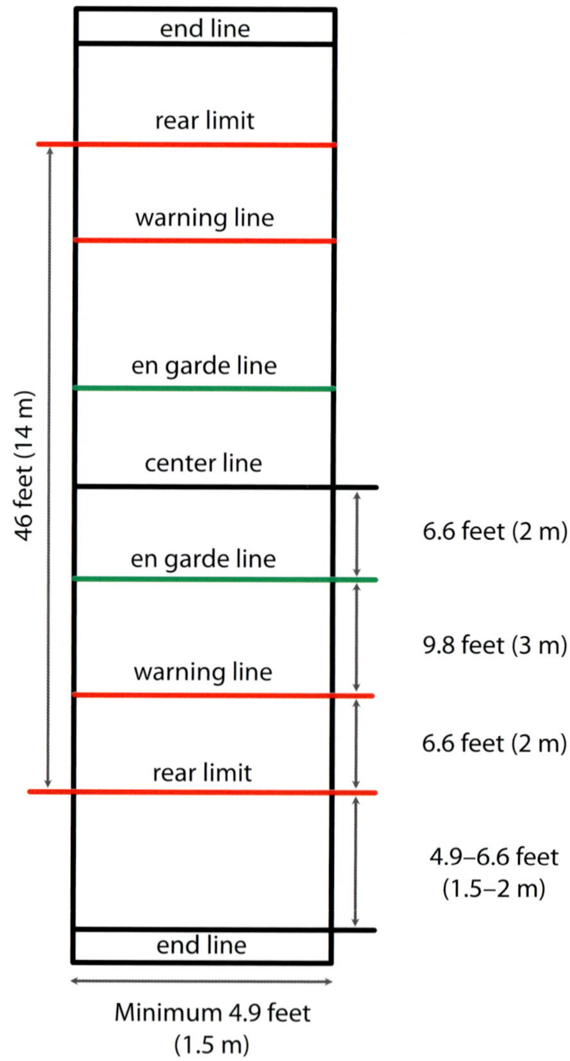

USA Fencing National Championships

In the United States, fencing competitions are under the supervision of an organization called USA Fencing. It has been holding the National Championships since 1892. USA Fencing holds multiple tournaments throughout the year. Each fencing season begins in the fall and includes both regional and national events.

Atlantic City, New Jersey

In the fall of 2024, 2,000 competitors from more than 40 states took part in the USA Fencing October North American Cup. This was the first event of the 2024–2025 season. It was held at the Atlantic City Convention Center.

Keeping Score

The goal of a fencing match, or bout, is to be the first to reach 15 points. Points are gained by making a touch with the fencing weapon in the opponent's target area. In épée and foil, there are time limits. Competitors fence for three rounds, or periods, of 3 minutes or 15 points each, with a minute to rest between rounds. In saber events, the first period lasts for 3 minutes or eight touches.

In some international competitions, fencers compete as a team. In these matches, each member of a three-person team faces each fencer from the other team over nine total bouts. Each bout lasts three minutes, or until one fencer scores a certain number of points.

Foil and saber bouts have a rule called right of way. If both fencers get a touch at the same time, the referee must decide who won. The fencer determined by the referee to have attacked first gets "right of way" and wins the bout. In épée, both fencers get a point instead.

The term *en garde* is a French phrase that means "on guard." It is the basic stance a fencer will take.

Referees will halt a bout if there is a safety issue. If fencers do not stop when the referee orders them to, they get a penalty. Penalties are also given if fencers **stall** or make a false start. If either fencer's equipment malfunctions during a bout, they get a penalty as well. If fencers intentionally strike the back of an opponent's head, they also receive a penalty.

A green or red light on electronic scoring equipment indicates that a fencer has scored a point. A white or yellow light means a touch did not hit the targeted area.

Fencing without electronic scoring equipment is called dry fencing. Four judges watch to see which competitor scores first.

Rules and Techniques

In a fencing bout, two fencers take their positions opposite each other on the piste. They stand unmasked behind the en-garde lines. Both fencers will salute their opponent, the referee, and spectators with their weapon. Then, the fencers put on their masks. The referee stands opposite the piste, facing the scoring box. The bout begins when the referee says *pret? Allez!* This is French for "Ready? Go!"

Points are scored when competitors hit the target area. In épée, competitors can target the whole body with the tip of their sword. In foil fencing, the target area does not include the arms, legs, or head. Saber fencers may target anywhere above the waist, but must connect with the edge of the saber, not the tip, to score a point.

Fencers begin each bout about 13 feet (4 m) apart from each other.

Fencers use several techniques to get a touch on their opponent. When a fencer wants to reach their opponent, they take a large step toward them. This is called a **lunge**. Opponents may **parry** attacks by deflecting them with their blade. They may also try to dodge their opponent's strike, or make a counterattack.

If there is a tie, fencers will have one minute to score a point to break it. If neither fencer scores, the bout is determined by a coin toss.

A referee will raise a card when fencers break rules. A yellow card is a warning, while a red card means the penalized fencer's opponent gets a point.

A fencer's weapon is inspected before a match. Fencers will often bring several weapons to the match, in case one fails an inspection.

Playing the Game

Most fencers are **amateurs**. They participate in college or town clubs. There are thousands of such clubs all over the world.

USA Fencing is in charge of amateur fencing in the United States. The organization helps people find clubs to join. Having a membership in USA Fencing allows amateur fencers to compete in regional, national, and international competitions.

Some people begin to learn fencing when they are as young as 7 years old.

USA Fencing oversees 600 fencing clubs around the country and numerous events each year.

Many U.S. fencing clubs are also members of the Fédération Internationale d'Escrime (FIE), or International Fencing Federation, the organization that makes the rules for fencing around the world. There are several international fencing competitions each year for professional fencers. Some competitions are for individuals, and others are for teams. These professional competitions include the Olympics, World Fencing Championships, Commonwealth Games, and the Asian Games.

People also take part in wheelchair fencing at the Paralympics. Olympic and Paralympic athletes are members of Team USA. This organization supports fencers and other athletes. Team USA provides mental and physical health assistance while also helping professional fencers find financial aid and training.

The best fencers are ranked according to points scored. Those with the most points are considered the best in their field. These athletes also often win gold, silver, or bronze medals at international competitions.

Team USA works with more than 4,500 athletes, including many fencers.

In total, 212 fencers from around the world competed in the 2024 Olympics.

History of Fencing

Fencing has gone from being a form of warfare to an elite sporting event. Over time, new technology has been introduced to bring the sport into the modern age.

Wheelchair fencing has been a part of the Paralympic Games since 1960.

1536 The fencing manual *Opera Nova*, by Achille Marozzo, is published in Italy. It helps make fencing more popular around the country.

1763 Italian fencing master Domenico Angelo establishes modern fencing techniques in his school in London. His book, *L'École des armes*, formalizes many techniques still in use today.

1896 Foil and saber fencing are included in the first modern Olympic Games, held in Athens.

1924 Female fencers take part in the Olympics for the first time when women's foil fencing becomes an official event at the Paris Olympics.

1933 Electronic scoring becomes part of épée competitions.

2024 Athletes from Cape Verde, Cyprus, Kenya, Niger, and Rwanda participate in fencing at the Olympic Games for the first time.

U.S.-trained fencers have won more than 30 medals at the Olympics.

In 1920, Douglas Fairbanks was the first actor to hire a fencing master so that sword fighting could be accurately depicted in movie scenes.

Fencing became a nationally organized sport in the United States in 1891.

Superstars of Fencing

Fencing has a long and storied past, with legendary players throughout its history.

Aladár Gerevich

BIRTH DATE: March 16, 1910
HOMETOWN: Jászberény, Hungary

CAREER FACTS:

- Over a 28-year period, Aladár won seven Olympic gold medals in fencing.
- Aladár is the first person to win an Olympic gold medal in the same sport in six different years.
- Solid saber skills helped Aladár win the world championship in saber three times.
- At age 50, Aladár was told he was too old to be part of Hungary's 1960 Olympic saber team. He defeated the entire Hungarian team to prove otherwise, and was allowed to compete.

Beatrice Vio

BIRTH DATE: March 4, 1997
HOMETOWN: Venice, Italy

CAREER FACTS:

- Beatrice began fencing at the age of 5. She continued to fence after her arms and legs had to be amputated because of an illness.
- At the Paralympics, Beatrice has won two gold medals, one silver medal, and three bronze medals.
- Beatrice has won both European Championships and World Championships.

Edoardo Mangiarotti

BIRTH DATE: April 7, 1919
HOMETOWN: Renate, Italy

CAREER FACTS:

- Edoardo won 13 Olympic medals, the most ever collected by a fencer.
- Edoardo won 26 World Championship medals, including 14 gold.
- At the 1952 Olympic Games, in Helsinki, Finland, Edoardo captured a gold épée medal and a silver foil medal.
- After retiring in 1961, Edoardo worked for the Italian Fencing Federation. He later served as the General Secretary of the FIE.

Mariel Zagunis

BIRTH DATE: March 3, 1985
HOMETOWN: Portland, Oregon

CAREER FACTS:

- Mariel is a two-time Olympic champion in the individual saber event.
- In 2004, when she was 19, Mariel became the first U.S. fencer to win an Olympic gold medal in 100 years.
- While competing in the World Championships, Mariel has won six gold, five silver, and five bronze medals in saber fencing.
- In 2013, Mariel became a member of the FIE Hall of Fame.

Lee Kiefer

BIRTH DATE: June 15, 1994
HOMETOWN: Lexington, Kentucky

CAREER FACTS:

- Lee began fencing at a young age after watching her father compete.
- Lee has won gold in two Olympic games.
- In 2018, Indiana's University of Notre Dame created the Lee Kiefer/Gerek Meinhardt Award, partially in her honor. It is presented to fencers who give their time selflessly and humbly in training.
- In 2022, Lee became a member of the FIE Hall of Fame.

Laura Flessel-Colovic

BIRTH DATE: November 6, 1971
HOMETOWN: Guadeloupe, France

CAREER FACTS:

- Known as "The Wasp," Laura is a five-time Olympic medalist in épée, including two golds.
- Laura won six medals at the European Championships, including individual gold in 2007.
- After retiring from fencing, Laura became the French Secretary of Sports.

Vivian Kong Man Wai

BIRTH DATE: February 8, 1994
HOMETOWN: Hong Kong

CAREER FACTS:

- Vivian began fencing when she was 11 years old.
- At the 2024 Olympic Games, Vivian won one gold medal.
- Vivian has won four gold, three silver, and four bronze World Cup medals in épée fencing.
- In épée Grand Prix events, Vivian won two gold, one silver, and two bronze medals.

Staying Healthy

Fencing is a fast-paced sport. It requires speed, endurance, and flexibility. Fencers need a strong **core**, legs, and upper body to perform the quick moves the sport demands. They exercise to keep themselves fit. This includes weight training, running, cycling, and swimming.

Proper nutrition is important for fencers. It helps them maintain their energy. Fencers focus on balanced meals that contain **carbohydrates** for energy, **protein** for healthy muscles, and fats. Water is also key, especially before and after training or a competition.

Fencers perform stretches before and after fencing. Light stretching helps them warm up muscles. It improves their flexibility, while reducing the risk of pulls or strains.

Sometimes, fencers get a sore elbow from using their sword arm. Stretching helps prevent this injury.

Eating kale and other leafy greens help fencers stay healthy.

Strengthening key muscle groups such as the legs, core, shoulders, and arms is important for fencers. Exercise help fencers move with precision. A well-balanced training program also helps prevent overuse injuries, which are caused by repeatedly using one part of the body. Fencers often focus on improving overall body stability and learning proper footwork techniques to avoid rolling ankles or knee injuries.

Fencers sweat a great deal due to their heavy uniforms. Drinking water helps them replace fluids lost while competing.

THE FENCING QUIZ

- 1 -

What are **three** weapons used in fencing?

- 2 -

What are **fencing masks** made from?

- 3 -

What type of fencing was officially recognized as a **sport** by the French Fencing Federation in 2019?

- 4 -

How many years of **training** do fencers need before competing professionally?

- 5 -

What is a **piste**?

- 6 -

What does ***en garde*** mean?

- 7 -

Which fencing event allows the whole body as a **target area**?

- 8 -

What **color** of card is considered a warning in fencing?

- 9 -

What type of **exercise** can prevent fencers from getting a sore elbow?

- 10 -

How old was **Beatrice Vio** when she began fencing?

ANSWERS: 1 The épée, foil, and saber 2 Wire mesh or stainless steel 3 Lightsaber fencing 4 Two to three 5 The area in which a fencing bout takes place 6 "On guard" 7 The épée 8 Yellow 9 Stretching 10 5

Key Words

amateurs: people who take part in something for fun

carbohydrates: sugars, starches, and other compounds found in food

civilizations: the cultures found in specific areas at specific times

core: the muscles in the middle of a person's torso

épée: a stiff-bladed, heavy fencing sword used for stabbing

foil: a flexible fencing sword used for stabbing

guard: part of the weapon between the handle and the blade that protects the fencer's hand

lunge: an attack in which fencers launch themselves at their opponent

mesh: something that forms a fine, netlike pattern

parry: to block a weapon by striking it with a weapon

protein: complex compounds found in foods such as meat

reels: spinning objects on which ropes or similar items can be wound

Renaissance: a period of time in Europe, from the 14th to 17th centuries, that is known for advancements in science and art

saber: a weapon used in fencing that can both slash and stab

stall: to delay the start of something

touches: when fencers score points by making contact with their opponent's target area with their weapon

Index

Get the best of both worlds.

AV2 bridges the gap between print and digital.

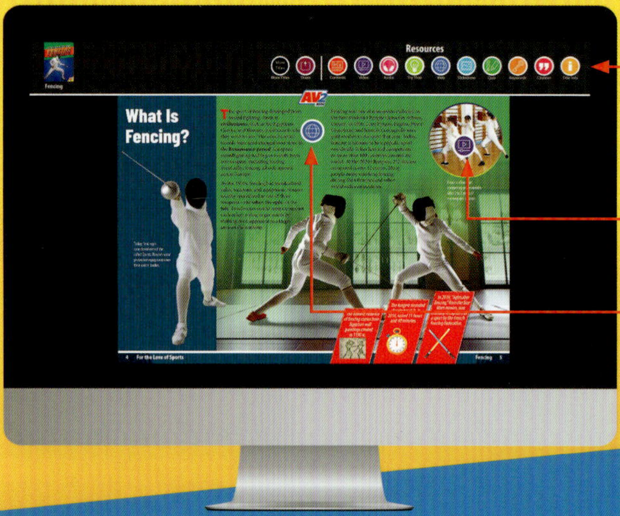

The expandable resources toolbar enables quick access to content including videos, audio, activities, **weblinks**, **slideshows**, **quizzes**, and **key words**.

Animated videos make static images come alive.

Resource icons on each page help readers to further **explore key concepts**.

Published by Lightbox Learning Inc.
276 5th Avenue, Suite 704 #917
New York, NY 10001
Website: www.openlightbox.com

Library of Congress Control Number: 2025931422

ISBN 979-8-8745-2639-9 (hardcover)
ISBN 979-8-8745-2640-5 (softcover)
ISBN 979-8-8745-2641-2 (static multi-user eBook)
ISBN 979-8-8745-2643-6 (interactive multi-user eBook)

Printed in Guangzhou, China
1 2 3 4 5 6 7 8 9 0 29 28 27 26 25

012025
101124

Project Coordinator John Willis
Art Director Terry Paulhus
Layout Jean Faye Rodriguez

Photo Credits
Every reasonable effort has been made to trace ownership and to obtain permission to reprint copyright material. The publisher would be pleased to have any errors or omissions brought to its attention so that they may be corrected in subsequent printings. The publisher acknowledges Alamy, Getty Images, Shutterstock, and Wikimedia as its primary image suppliers for this title.